MUZIO CLEMENTI was born in Rome in the year 1752. His father was a worker in gold and silver, who recognized the uncommon musical talent of his son and put him under the instruction of Buroni, a Roman organist. Other teachers followed Buroni. Cordicelli taught Muzio thorough-bass; Carpani gave him lessons in counterpoint; and Santarelli was his singing-master. When he was nine years old he discharged the duties of a church organist, and by the time that he was fourteen he was famous in his native town as a performer and a composer. He then fell in with a wealthy amateur of music, an Englishman named Bedford (or, as Marmontel has it, Sir Beckford). This Englishman in time persuaded the father to intrust his son to him, promising that the boy should have rare advantages and a most favorable introduction into the musical society of London. This promise was fully kept, and until 1770 Clementi lived with his patron in a country-house in Dorsetshire; he was cared for tenderly; and he studied with zeal the works of Handel, Bach, D. Scarlatti, and Paradies. In 1770 he published his first sonata, and appeared with brilliant success in London as pianist and composer. From 1777 until 1780 he was cembalist at the Italian Opera in that city, and in 1781 he started on his travels. He gave concerts in Paris, where he also played before Marie Antoinette; and then he went to Vienna by way of Strasburg and Munich. In Vienna he played in friendly rivalry with Mozart before the Emperor Joseph II. In 1785 he made another visit to Paris, but with this exception he remained in London until 1802. He was conductor, virtuoso, composer and teacher. He grew rich, but he lost heavily by the failure of a pianoforte and music-publishing house. This loss led him to found a similar business. In 1802 he went with John Field, his favorite pupil, to St. Petersburg, via Paris and Vienna. Spohr met him there, and gives an amusing account of finding him washing his stockings because the washerwomen of the town were "incompetent and extortionary." Clementi then stopped at Berlin and Dresden and gave lessons. He was married in Berlin, and his wife died within the year following. Sick at heart, he went to St. Petersburg with his pupils, Klengel and Berger. In 1810 he returned to England by way of Vienna and Italian towns. He passed the rest of his days in England, with the exception of a visit to the Continent in 1820-21, when he spent the winter at Leipzig, where he was courted by all; three of his symphonies were played under his direction, and he was presented with a cup of Meissner porcelain bearing a Latin inscription. He lived to be eighty years old, and died at Evesham, near London, March 10th, 1832. His eye was not dim, nor his natural force abated. He was married thrice, and had children in his old age; and although after 1810 he played little in public and devoted himself to composition and business, yet shortly before his death he made such men as Cramer and Moscheles marvel at the display of his technique and the richness and fire of his improvisation. He lies buried in the south cloister of Westminster Abbey.

The career of Clementi was remarkably free from the adventures, the disappointments, the reverses, that are so often connected with the artistic life. It was so free from romance that the biographers of the last century felt obliged to invent incidents of passion. He was a favorite in society, for his manners were elegant, and he was always a cheerful and entertaining companion. He enjoyed a game of billiards, but he was frugal in his habits. He was exceedingly fond of money, and many amusing stories are told of his stinginess. He was industrious, and often gave fifteen hour-lessons a day at a guinea a lesson. It is unnecessary to add that by teaching, playing, composing, improvements in the pianoforte, and a diligent pursuit of business, he was able to leave a large fortune.

As player and composer, Clementi may be justly regarded as the founder of modern pianoforte-playing. In 1790 Gerber called him "the greatest and the only clavierist." Forty years later, as a pianist, although then very old, he was listened to eagerly and with enthusiasm by the greatest pianists of the day. It is true that Mozart called him a charlatan, and Dittersdorf found more mechanical skill than true art in his performance; but Mozart hated the Italians and was given to violent language. It must also be remembered that when he played first in Vienna, he had accustomed himself to the instrument of the day, and, according to his own account, he had cultivated "a brilliant execution, especially in double stops, hardly known then, and in extemporized cadenzas, and had subsequently achieved a more melodic and noble style of performance after listening attentively to famous singers, and also by means of the perfected mechanism of English pianos, the construction of which formerly stood in the way of a cantabile and legato style of playing." It is said on the best of authority that no one ever possessed in like degree his marvelous equality of fingers, or the clearness and finish that characterized his fugue-playing, wherein each part had "the sonority, the accent and the *timbre* proper to it in the musical discourse." His hands were quiet, the wonderfully agile and independent fingers doing all the work; the smoothness of the legato was as remarkable as the brilliancy of his playing.

The roll of his pupils includes these names: John Field, J. B. Cramer, Zeuner, Klengel, Bertini, Kalkbrenner, Berger, Meyerbeer, and Moscheles.

He composed 106 pianoforte sonatas (46 of them with violin, 'cello and flute), the "Gradus ad Parnassum," symphonies, overtures, caprices, duos, character-pieces; and he edited a valuable collection of pianoforte-works by the old masters. As a composer he is remarkable, first of all, in this: That although Handel was alive when he was born, and although Beethoven died before him, he preserved throughout his life his own artistic individuality, which was nourished by close communion with the greatest composers of the old Italian and the old German school. Not without reason has Riehl called him, "the master of the sonata." Beethoven himself valued these sonatas highly, for their spontaneity, their terse and accurate form, their incitement to an artistic treatment of the instrument for which they were written. Some of the earlier ones in their breadth hint at the Beethoven of later years. The study of these pure works, that abound in ingenious detail, cannot be too highly recommended. As for the "Gradus," published in 1817, it forms to-day the foundation of pianoforte-playing. The elder Marmontel does not exceed the bounds of critical judgment in saying: "It offers to serious pupils, to all artists devoted to the highest art, the most beautiful models of taste, the choicest examples of all styles, the noble, the severe, the graceful, the expressive, the pathetic. The studies devoted especially to mechanism, rhythm, and ornamentation are as admirably conceived for acquiring independence of the fingers and freedom of pace; and the rules are laid down by Clementi with unerring precision." PHILIP HALE.

SCHIRMER'S LIBRARY
OF MUSICAL CLASSICS

Vol. 40

MUZIO CLEMENTI

Op. 36, 37, 38

Sonatinas

For the Piano

Revised and Fingered by

LOUIS KOEHLER

With a Biographical Sketch of the Author by

PHILIP HALE

ISBN 978-0-7935-5173-6

G. SCHIRMER, Inc.

DISTRIBUTED BY

HAL•LEONARD
CORPORATION
7777 W. BLUEMOUND RD. P.O. BOX 13819 MILWAUKEE, WI 53213

Printed in the U.S.A. by G. Schirmer, Inc.

Index.

SONATINA.

Op. 36, № 1.

Spiritoso.

M. CLEMENTI.

Printed in the U.S.A. by G. Schirmer, Inc.

SONATINA.

Op. 36, Nº 2.

Allegretto.

2.

Allegro.

SONATINA.

Op. 36, No 3.

Spiritoso.

3.

Un poco adagio

Allegro

SONATINA.

Op. 36, N.º 4.

Con spirito.

4.

Andante con espressione.

Rondo
Allegro vivace

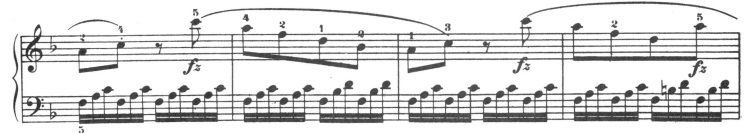

Da Capo al Fine.

SONATINA.
Op. 36, No. 5.

Air Suisse (Original.)

Allegro moderato.

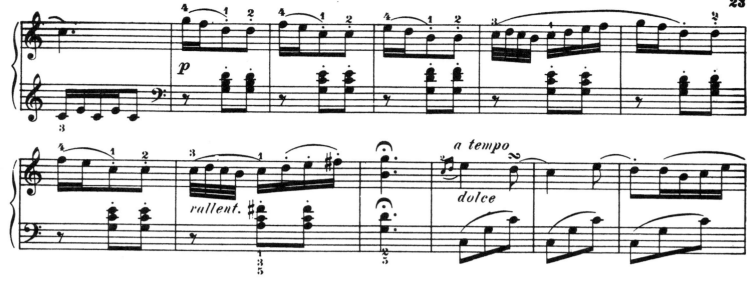

Rondo
Allegro di molto

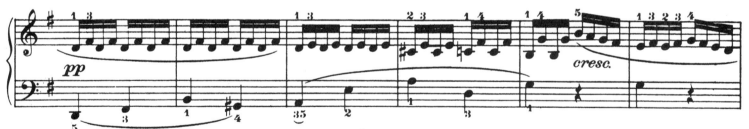

SONATINA.

Op. 36, No 6.

Allegro con spirito.

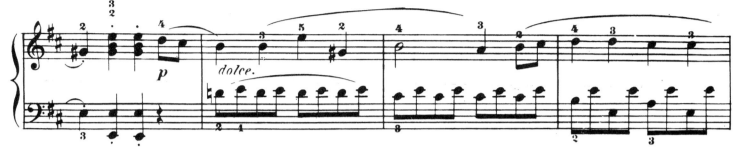

Rondo.
Allegretto spiritoso

SONATINA.

Op. 37, № 1.

Andantino.

p con espressione.

7.

Presto.

SONATINA.
Op. 37, No 2.

Allegro assai.

8.

Menuetto.

Men. *da capo, senza replica.*

SONATINA.

Op. 37, Nº 3.

Allegro e spirituoso.

9.

Allegro.

Minore.

Maggiore.

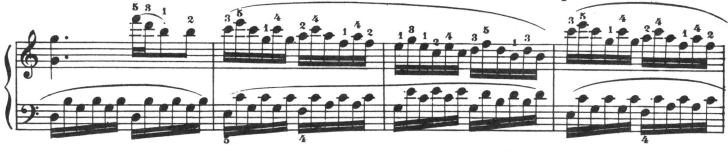

SONATINA.

Op. 38, № 1.

Allegro.

10.

Tempo di Menuetto.
Andantino.

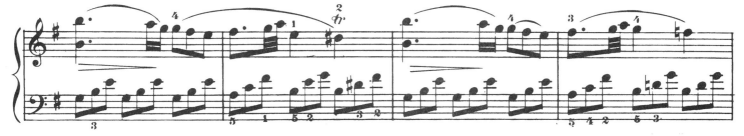

SONATINA.

Op.38, № 2.

Allegro moderato.

11.

Rondo.
Allegretto.

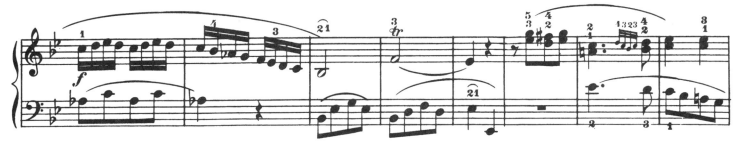

SONATINA.
Op.38, №3.

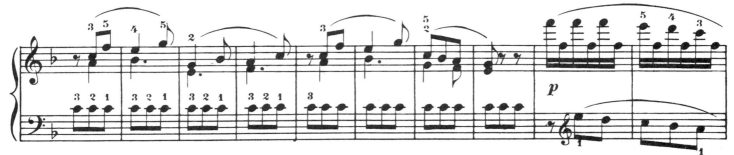